Focus on Fine Arts:

HUMANITIES

(A Case Study)

Thomas Rooney

Frederick B. Tuttle, Jr.
Series Editor

nea **PROFESSIONAL LIBRARY**
National Education Association
Washington, D.C.

Printing History
First Printing: September 1989

Note

The opinions expressed in this publication should not be construed as representing the policy or position of the National Education Association. Materials
published by the NEA Professional Library are intended to be discussion documents for educators who are concerned with specialized interests of the
profession.

Library of Congress Cataloging-in-Publication Data

Rooney, Thomas.
      Humanities : a case study / Thomas Rooney.
         p.   cm. — (Focus on fine arts)
      Bibliography: p.
      ISBN 0-8106-0302-0
      1. Arts—Study and teaching—United States—Case studies.
   I. Title.   II. Series.
   NX303.R66   1989
   700'.7'1273—dc19   89-30994
                                                              CIP

CONTENTS

The Author

Thomas Rooney is a teacher of English and Humanities at Needham High School, Massachusetts.

The Series Editor

Frederick B. Tuttle, Jr., is Assistant Superintendent, Needham Public Schools, Massachusetts. A former university professor and education consultant, Dr. Tuttle is the author of *Composition: A Media Approach, Gifted and Talented Students,* and *How to Prepare Students for Writing Tests;* the editor of *Fine Arts in the Curriculum;* and the coauthor of *Technical and Scientific Writing, Characteristics and Identification of Gifted and Talented Students,* and *Program Design and Development for Gifted and Talented Students,* all published by NEA. He also developed the NEA multimedia program *Educating Gifted and Talented Students.*

The Advisory Panel

Peter Huybers, Social Studies Teacher, Hillside Junior High School, Simi Valley, California

Barbara A. Johnson, Humanities and English Teacher, Russellville High School, Arkansas

Robert A. Lague, Drama and Music Teacher, Andover High School, Massachusetts

Sharon A. Rasor, Assistant Professor of Music, Wright State University, Dayton, Ohio

EDITOR'S PREFACE

> American people are today concerned with hu-
> manistic and cultural matters to a degree un-
> precedented in their history. [Far] from reflecting
> this new concern with humanistic and cultural
> matters, the schools of the nation have let the
> humanities and the arts languish. (10)*

THE ARTS ARE BASIC

The position of the performing and visual arts in our educational system has not improved appreciably since Alvin Eurich made
this observation in 1969. While few would deny the value of the
arts, many continually relegate them to the periphery of curricula
in most schools. In 1985 the national Parent Teachers Association
found that—

> Nearly 70 percent of the 1,164 schools recently surveyed by the Alli-
> ance of Independent Colleges of Art have experienced cuts in art
> teachers, courses or program budgets since 1981. Forty percent of
> these schools expect even further cuts.
> Only about 2 percent of the average school budget is spent on arts
> programs. . . .
> Knowledge and skills in music have decreased by 3.3 percent
> among 9-year-olds and 2.5 percent among 17-year-olds in the past
> seven years. (10)

To effect a substantive change we need not only a reaffirmation of
the importance of the arts, but also practical descriptions of ways
that they can begin to fulfill their roles in the educational process.
The National Endowment for the Arts gives direction to this need:

> Basic arts education must give students the essence of our civilization,
> the civilizations which have contributed to ours, and the more distant
> civilizations which enrich world civilizations as a whole. It must also
> give students tools for creating, for communicating and understanding
> others' communications, and for making informal and critical choices.
> (9, p. 13)

Importance of the Arts

Education in the arts plays a major role in three general areas of

---

*Numbers in parentheses appearing in this Preface refer to the References on page 11.

5

educational impact: societal, instructional, and individual. "[One] of the major goals of education should be to promote the continuation of culture, transmitting values and concepts of civilization from one generation to the next" (13). Through study of the arts we may acquire a cultural record of our past and present. This understanding is necessary to help put ourselves and our value systems into perspective. The necessity of such a perspective has been acknowledged by William Bennett, former secretary of education:

> All students, then, should know some of these works [of art] for a simple reason: they cannot understand the present if they have no understanding of the past. If we cut them off from our culture's past, we automatically make youth aliens in their own culture. And that makes them ill-equipped to succeed in or even understand the world around them. (3)

While students gain knowledge of events and historical movements that shaped society, they also gain insights into the underlying value systems and beliefs of societies and cultures through the arts. "[Humans] experience and give expression to their most deeply held values, beliefs, and images through the arts, and there can be no adequate form of general education that does not include them" (12).

Instructionally, the arts may provide both creative outlets for students to express themselves as well as alternative avenues through which students may understand others' feelings and ideas. Some teachers base their interpretations of a student's learnings primarily on performance on "objective" tests, written essays, or class participation. However, many students who do not perform well through these means are able to show that they understand a concept when encouraged to respond through other means such as art, photography, drama, and dance (14). Ultimately, students must learn how to communicate effectively through tests and essays if they are to succeed in our educational system. But some students must first acquire confidence in themselves. Once they are able to demonstrate that they do understand the concepts, these students often transfer this confidence to responses through other, more "academic," means. Indeed, once a student shows understanding of a concept, the instructional task changes. Instead of stressing the concept itself, the teacher may then focus on the mode of expression.

Moreover, some students learn particular concepts more effectively through the arts than through textbooks and lectures. While developing a program using films and pictures to teach poetry, for example, I found that many students for whom the poems were considered too difficult could accurately state the themes of the poems when they were presented visually in films. I concluded that "once the students have found they can read visual images accompanying a poem, they can [often] read and react critically to the poem itself [in its printed version]" (15). Robert Spillane, Superintendent of Fairfax County (Virginia) Public Schools, summarizes the importance of the arts to all education:

In any case, an education and a life that ignore vast areas of expression, communication, conceptualization, and innovation—the visual and aural areas—will surely hamstring our future communicators, conceptualizers, and innovators. . . . Thus, education must give space—albeit in a crowded curriculum—to the arts, which connect thinking and feeling in the aural and visual worlds. (12).

The inability of students and teachers to draw connections among disciplines has resulted in a fragmentation of learning. As students progress from one grade level to the next, this isolation of studies increases. Ernest Boyer, President of the Carnegie Foundation for the Advancement of Teaching, comments on the role arts education may play in overcoming this departmentalization of learning:

After visiting colleges and schools, I am convinced that students at all levels need to see connections. And I believe that finding patterns across separate disciplines can be accomplished through the arts. . . . I'm suggesting that the arts give us a language that cuts across the disciplines, help us to see connections and bring a more coherent meaning to our world. (4)

Perhaps the greatest benefit of arts education is to the student as an individual. The "arts can provide the means for communicating thoughts, emotions, and ideas that cannot otherwise be expressed. The arts also contribute significantly to each individual's search for identity, self-realization, and personal confidence" (12). One of the outcomes of the "visual literacy" movement in the 1970s was the introduction of filmmaking as part of many curricula. Students who had previously considered dropping out of school began to use film to share their ideas and feelings with teachers and classmates. They became recognized and valued in the academic envi-

7

ronment because they could interact effectively with others. For the first time they encountered success instead of failure in school. Boyer places this role of the arts at the top of his list: "First, the arts are needed in the nation's schools because they help children express feelings and ideas words cannot convey" (4).

For those students who have particular aptitude in the arts, the inclusion of the arts in education is especially vital. As Elliot Eisner, Professor of Art and Education at Stanford University, observes,

> The inclusion of the arts in the school's curriculum provides opportunity not only for all students to learn to read the arts, but especially for those students whose aptitudes are in the arts. . . . It is hard to discover what one doesn't have an opportunity to practice. Educational equity is an empty ideal when a substantial portion of our children are excluded from the very areas in which their talents reside. (6)

Although the importance of the arts in education has been generally acknowledged for these and other reasons, in most schools the arts are still treated as "frill" areas of the curriculum with the basic instruction focusing on language, mathematics, science, and social studies. When a budget crisis strikes, as it did in California with Proposition 13 and in Massachusetts with Proposition 2 1/2, arts education usually suffers through severe budget cuts or even elimination. Eisner offers several reasons for the marginal position of arts in the curriculum. Among these are views that (1) the arts are emotional, not cognitive; (2) lack of assessment in the arts; (3) the arts are solely creative experiences; and (4) the arts are innate rather then learned (6). To place education in the arts closer to the center of the curriculum, we must address these views and realistically demonstrate vital roles the arts may play within academic curricula. As Bennett states, "Those of us engaged in education must promote the truth that study of the arts increases both our individual capacities for creativity and love for the highest creative work of others" (2).

Underlying Assumptions for the Fine Arts Series

The basic premise for developing this series of monographs on the arts in the classroom is that to accomplish the preservation and transmission of knowledge, skill, values, and culture from generation to generation, we must address the study of the humanities, including the study of visual and performing arts. Four assumptions underlie this premise:

1. All students should have both exposure to and instruction in visual and performing arts throughout elementary and secondary education.
2. Curricula in the visual and performing arts should be presented both as unique disciplines in themselves as well as integral components of other disciplines where appropriate.
3. As with any discipline, visual and performing arts curricula should follow a sequential, organized pattern from kindergarten through grade 12.
4. Finally, the effectiveness of programs and student achievement in visual and performing arts should be assessed based on the program and content of the curricula.

Instruction should not be limited only to those students who display particular talents in the arts. As the National PTA states: "Art is basic to life. It helps us understand ourselves and others. It provides comfort and pleasure through books, music, film, painting and the performing and decorative arts" (10). All students should have the opportunity to enjoy and learn from the arts. Exposure alone is not sufficient, however. "Appreciating a work of art demands intelligent application of perceptual and cognitive resources" (11). Such learning calls for direct instruction.

This instruction should be developmental and sequential from elementary through secondary school, with each year building upon learnings of a previous year. Describing the Discipline-Based Art Education program, Eisner states:

> If a sound art education program were implemented effectively in schools from kindergarten through twelfth grade, youngsters finishing school would be more artistically literate.... Youngsters finishing schooling would understand something about the relationships between culture and the content and form of art. (5)

Too often many educators treat art education as either a separate study isolated from other disciplines or only in relation to other disciplines. Both approaches are necessary for students to learn the content of visual and performing arts as well as the integral relationships between the arts and other disciplines. While the visual and performing arts are disciplines in themselves with their own

9

contents, they are also integral to many other disciplines. When studied in support of other disciplines, however, the arts tend to be viewed only as illustrations of concepts in the more "academic" studies, with little attention being paid to their own content. Consequently, education in the arts should be approached in both ways: as separate disciplines and in relation to other disciplines.

Unless the effectiveness of arts programs is legitimately assessed, work in those curricula will not be highly valued. As Eisner observes, "What we test is what we teach" (6). Consequently, program evaluation should assess the validity of the content, the effectiveness of instruction and, especially, student achievement. Since most student achievement in the visual and performing arts does not lend itself to traditional evaluation procedures, many arts educators base their evaluation on effort rather than actual achievement. As with other disciplines, however, students should be held to appropriate standards and expectations related directly to the instruction and content. In Project Zero, for example, which emphasizes student production, the assessment procedures focus on projects, portfolios, and interviews concentrating on the students' creative processes (8, 15). In the Discipline-Based Arts Education program, "Evaluation of outcomes pertains not only to the products of the students' efforts—the skills, the newfound appreciations, the fresh understandings, the refined judgment that students achieve—but also to the way in which students are engaged in the process of learning" (6). Each program should design its own assessment procedure based on the content of the discipline and the goals of the instructional approach. In the report *Toward Civilization,* the National Endowment for the Arts stresses the importance of assessment in the arts: "Without testing and evaluation, there is no way to measure individual and program progress, program objectives will lack specificity, the arts courses will continue to be considered extracurricular and unimportant" (9, p. 27).

—Frederick B. Tuttle, Jr.
Series Editor

REFERENCES

1. "Arts Education: A Position Statement and Proposed Action." Boston: Board of Education, Commonwealth of Massachusetts, 1975.

2. Bennett, William J. "The Flap." Speech given at National Association of Schools of Music National Convention, Colorado Springs, Colorado, November 24, 1986.

3. _____."Why the Arts Are Essential." *Educational Leadership* 45, no. 4, January 1988.

4. Boyer, Ernest L. *"The Arts, Language and the Schools."* Basic Education 2, no. 4, Summer 1987.

5. Eisner, Elliot. "On Discipline-Based Art Education: A Conversation with Elliot Eisner." *Educational Leadership* 45, no. 4, January 1988.

6. _____. *The Role of Discipline-Based Art Education in America's Schools.* Los Angeles: Getty Center for Education in the Arts, 1986.

7. _____. "Why Arts Are Basic." *Basic Education* 31, no. 9, May 1987.

8. Gardner, Howard. "On Assessment in the Arts: A Conversation with Howard Gardner." *Educational Leadership* 45, no. 4, January 1988.

9. National Endowment for the Arts. *Toward Civilization: A Report on Arts Education.* Washington, D.C.: U.S. Government Printing Office, May 1988.

10. National Parent Teachers Association. *Children and the Arts: What Your PTA Can Do.* Chicago: the Association, 1985.

11. Perkins, D. N. "Art as an Occasion of Intelligence." *Educational Leadership* 45, no. 4, January 1988.

12. Spillane, Robert R. "Arts Education Is Not a Frill." Updating School Board Policies. Alexandria, Va.: National School Boards Association, 1987.

13. Tuttle, Frederick B., Jr. ed. *Fine Arts in the Curriculum.* Washington, D.C.: National Education Association, 1985.

14. _____. "Robert's Problem . . . or Ours?—Visuals in the Classroom." *Connecticut English Journal,* Fall 1978.

15. _____. "Visualizing Poetry." *Media and Methods,* May 1970.

16. Wise, Joseph. "Music as a Catalyst for Inter-Disciplinary Education: Attitudes of School Administrators." *ERS Spectrum* 5, no. 2, Spring 1987.

17. Wolf, Dennie Palmer. "Opening Up Assessment." *Educational Leadership* 45, no. 4, January 1988

INTRODUCTION

Since the publication of *Fine Arts in the Curriculum* (10),*
many more educators and artists have expressed agreement with
the views of its contributors. For many years idealistic educators
and artists have declared the need for the arts in our lives as individuals and as a society. Once we begin to discuss the arts, we see
how basic they are to education as well as to life. We see that their
part in the curriculum must be much more than just "enrichment
activities." They must be at the heart of the curriculum, inspiring
its content and its process.

John Goodlad and Jack Morrison have asserted that "individuals
are deprived" and "society is the poorer when it fails to develop
both sensitive, attuned human beings and talented persons to en-
rich the lives for us all" (7). Because "we do not yet have a society
that assumes the full development of human character, with all its
richness and complexity, simply by growing up in it... deliberate
educational processes are required." The arts must be incorporated
in education to "challenge that part of the brain not actively engaged by many other kinds of stimuli." More than this, the arts
are the vehicles for creativity in the whole curriculum, for all learning. "The arts can be the *prime* vehicle for general education.... The story of civilization can best be understood through
studying the literature, drama, music, dance and visual arts of previous eras and by reinterpreting the human condition through contemporary participation in the arts" (7).

In their Briefing Paper for the Arts Education Community, a
group of artists point out the current dilemma of

> discriminating from an intellectual base...in matters of culture....
> Most Americans are not artistically literate to an extent that permits per-
> sonal discrimination about works of art on purely artistic grounds: "I
> don't know anything about art but I know what I like" is a commonly
> heard phrase. This situation leads us, both individually and in the ag-
> gregate, to a loss of distinction between art and entertainment.... If we

---

*Numbers in parentheses appearing in the text refer to the Bibliography on page 55.

lose the concept of distinction between the two, we lose the basis of discrimination about the relative purposes and values of aesthetic materials. At its extreme, such a condition creates an impossible context for providing rationales in support of serious arts education programs at the K–12 level. . . .America is a competitive society, a technological society, and a materialistic society. These conditions contribute powerfully to the development of American values about education. As is the case with art, the majority of Americans view education as a means to an end rather than as an end in itself. One becomes educated primarily in order to pursue a livelihood in a highly complex society. The idea of a life of the mind does not seem prominent either in our educational system or in our overall values about education. . . .Given the value system most people have about the arts, it is impossible for them to understand how serious study of the arts can produce the same capabilities [as study of mathematics, language, history, and science]. This is because most individuals do not understand what the content of study in the arts disciplines is, nor do they comprehend what kind of knowledge such study imparts beyond the acquisition of techniques for performing or making art. (8, pp. 6–7)

Not surprisingly, it is an art teacher, Jon Murray, who points out the importance of dealing with all learning the way students in art classes do. When "children make art," he says, they learn "to perceive, to distinguish, to organize, to form concepts, to express, to understand. . . .All artists and scientists realize that what we know depends on what we see; and what we see depends on *how* we see" (9, p. 23). This is not just true of small children:

Adolescence . . . is an important time to develop the ability to think abstractly, to consider abstract concepts and qualities apart from particular, concrete situations. In art class, as in English class, students learn to manipulate and express abstract ideas by working with them firsthand. They come to recognize the abstract qualities of all art, and learn that if they do not understand the paintings of Piet Mondrian, they will not really understand those of Jan Vermeer.

With good high-school art instruction, students can learn to see much more than likeness, just as with good literary instruction, they can learn to read much more than plot. They learn how to analyze the structure of a work and to see how this structure contributes to its meaning. They separate the work into its parts—sentences or lines, paragraphs or shapes, sounds or colors—and they figure out how these parts relate to one another to form a coherent, significant whole. By analyzing Shakespeare and Michelangelo, students learn how to admire and appreciate; but by analyzing their own works, they learn how to grow. (9, p. 24)

Murray finds that the qualities colleges ask high school teachers to consider when rating students ("curiosity, initiative, originality, self-direction, creativity, and the capacity to think and act independently") are

nurtured more in art than in any other subject area. In art class, more students spend more active learning time doing more different kinds of thinking: intuiting, imagining, recalling, interpreting, reasoning, abstracting, analyzing, organizing, applying, relating, synthesizing, expressing, and evaluating. More than any other activity, art challenges the whole student—intellectually, emotionally, and physically—to learn by doing. (9, p. 26)

Murray bemoans the "self-perpetuating lack of knowledge about art...visual illiteracy and the consequent undervaluing of the arts...thus passed along in institutionalized form" (9, p. 28). Fortunately educators have been trying to change the situation. The Educational EQuality Project of the College Entrance Examination Board in 1983 proposed a core curriculum that would give college-bound students the following background in the arts:

The ability to understand and appreciate the unique qualities of each of the arts; the ability to appreciate how people of various cultures have used the arts to express themselves; the ability to understand and appreciate different artistic styles and works from representative historical periods and cultures; some knowledge of the social and intellectual influences affecting artistic form; the ability to use the skills, media, tools, and processes required to express themselves in one or more of the arts... [and] "intensive preparation" in at least one art form... visual arts, theater, music, and dance. (6, p. 59)

How do such informed and idealistic suggestions become reality? Murray's suggestion that art be used as a model for other subjects might be part of the first step toward truly integrating the arts with other disciplines and ultimately unifying the whole curriculum. In explaining "Why Arts Are Basic," Elliot Eisner sees many virtues of effective arts education that are quite basic:

In the arts, choice is always multiple; the difference, however, is that there is rarely a single certain answer. Hence, when well taught the arts free the mind from rigid certainty. What could be more critical to any society seeking multiple solutions to the myriad problems before it? And such processes are of central importance in developing in citizens the tolerance and taste for coping with ambiguities and uncertain-

15

ties of human affairs... an inability to cope with diverse and at times conflicting visions about what is right, good or beautiful is the surest path to tyranny.... The absence of attention to the arts in our schools will result in an inability for most of our citizens to deal with more than "Wheel of Fortune," "As the World Turns," and "Dallas." After all, people "read" what they can. This brings us to another major aim of arts education: that through them children find meaningful access to their cultural heritage. Without such literacy that heritage itself will molder as skeletons in an unopened closet. The arts require a seeing eye in order to live. (5)

Arthur Efland looks for a more comprehensive kind of literacy so that the curriculum would deal "with more than verbal and mathematical symbols" (4); and Laura Chapman outlines such a curriculum with three main branches—the arts, the sciences, and the humanities (3). The first step toward these greater curricula is to see the natural relationship *between* the arts and the humanities. History, philosophy, religion, and other studies of societies and cultures go hand in hand with the arts. Arts educators certainly see their role in the context of "cultural formation":

This process is going on all the time in many settings and circumstances whether or not the arts education community is or has a chance to be involved. Since individual skills and knowledge in the aggregate define culture, the ultimate success of the arts education community rests primarily on its ability to intervene positively in the cultural formation process as it takes place in individual lives. ...What influence does formal education in the arts or in any discipline have in the formation of long-term cultural values? For too many Americans the [commercial broadcast] media prevail over all other influences. ...There are two fundamentally different approaches to cultural formation. One involves providing a continuous invitation to the individual to develop his or her understanding by enlarging his or her personal knowledge. The other involves constant attempts to wed the individual to the mass through psychological action. Cultural formation due to continuous application of mass psychological techniques is not possible through the electronic media. While these techniques have the power to generate interest, funding, and even psychological dependency that could increase support for the arts, it is clear that mass psychological action is an opposite concept to the nurturing of individual thought and spirit traditionally considered central to creation, presentation and reception of the arts. (8, p. 4)

The need to study the arts with the humanities seems urgent in a society saturated with the mass media. Of course the arts and the humanities have always been related. As Efland says, "In past societies they were bound up with religion; in the monarchies of Europe they glorified the ruler as the symbol of the state; in Marxist countries they function as propaganda; but thankfully, no set of officially dictated purposes yet governs their use in our society" (4, p. 12). Indeed, the arts give us the total picture of past and present, and—with monarchies and Marxism in mind—they serve as our defense against totalitarianism.

Ernest Boyer echoes this need; he recommends that the high school curriculum give literature and the arts top priority for every student, not just the college bound,

> to transmit the heritage of a people and express human joys and sorrows. They are the means by which a civilization can be measured. It is not accidental that dictators, who seek to control the minds and hearts of men, suppress not just the written and spoken word, but music, dance, and the visual arts, as well. . . .The arts are an essential part of the human experience. They are not a frill. We recommend that all students study the arts to discover how human beings use nonverbal symbols and communicate not only with words but through music, dance, and the visual arts. . . .Now, more than ever, all people need to see clearly, hear acutely, and feel sensitively through the arts. These skills are no longer just desirable. They are essential if we are to survive together with civility and joy. (2)

The purpose of this monograph is to present a rationale not merely for integrating the arts into secondary education but also for refocusing, for changing the manner in which we teach our students about history and the arts and the manner in which they experience the arts and other expressions of our culture and other cultures. Various approaches to curriculum are presented, with suggestions for equipping students to respond to works of art, to relate patterns in history to the arts, and to relate the styles and movements of the past to those of today.

Chapter 1

WHY A HUMANITIES COURSE?

Few American high school students know art or music history. Indeed, millions of American adults lack the experience, the skills, the knowledge to make educated choices about the art forms that surround, even bombard, them every day. The languages of the arts should not be foreign to anyone. Though politics and prejudice have often held the arts and people captive, by freeing the arts we help keep people free. Art is comprehensible as it is limited or defined according to systems that are familiar. These systems—religious, political, economic, social—impose their vocabularies and values on the artist. By studying the systems related to each piece of art we encounter, however, we can find the means to get close to the artist, to find something of ourselves in the work. When we study other areas of the humanities, other human expressions and systems—religion, politics, philosophy—we see that all the humanities are one, inseparable from one another and from us.

Every student can approach the arts through some aspect, depending on the individual's interests. For example, the student anthropologist or social scientist will want to study the function of the work. The student artist will see how the function will dictate the form of the work. The most literal students, as well as the historians in the class, will be most interested in the subject matter, the histories or legends or myths. We are all attracted by the form, by the images, the sounds, the movements themselves. Even to say we are "attracted" is to philosophize and to discuss why we are attracted. More basically, we all create forms. This is part of being human. From birth, we are involved in the creative process. We move, cry, build, fashion, imitate; constantly we give shape to our expression. Thus we are attracted to these forms by our human nature. The forms and expressions of creativity result from basic functions and needs. Because it is so natural to create, we can even create forms that we cannot understand. To understand our own actions is not simple, but it is part of growth and education. To learn how to discuss the works of other human beings is part of learning to understand what we ourselves do, too. Consequently, we must reflect upon the greatest human expressions. So it is with the other areas of the humanities—religion, history, philosophy, archaeology—all human expressions, creations of beliefs and values.

Studying human expressions of any kind is a struggle against many obstacles—biases, misunderstandings, stereotypes, clichés, oversimplifications. Our alliances and emotions get in the way of our objectivity as we confuse substance with style. In art, however, we can have the relief of objectivity; we can judge the work separately from the artist. We can "tell the dancer from the dance," the singer from the song, even the choreographer's form and style from the dancer's, the composer's, the singer's.

To which works of art do teachers have an obligation to expose their students? Must the choice be based on teachers' biases and tastes? Educators must bear in mind what students should know to be "equipped" to enjoy and understand the arts on their own. Thus, teachers must choose works that will lead to discussions of how various traditions and styles developed, great works that will, upon being seen, read, heard, prompt students to care about such discussions. Traditional "mainstreams" must be defined, and works outside the mainstream must not be ignored so that students will become aware of the relationship of the arts to the societies from which they come, including the economic and political structures that produced them, strengthened them, spread them, enforced them, or censored them.

Although some students may consider history to be nothing more than facts in chronological order, it should be taught as an exploration of human endeavors and expressions. History provides the framework to help us learn the changing forms, styles, and functions of the arts, religion, philosophy, and other humanistic endeavors. The study of history enhances the study of the arts, just as the study of the arts enhances the study of history. History helps find the "truth" or at least the zeitgeist of times and places. The best "liberal arts" courses bring historians, sociologists, and artists together to create the feeling of a time and place. Written history, though, whether of governments, science, art, or music gives us only a glimpse of the distorted "truths" because of biases and limited perceptions. Students and teachers must always question the situation, asking why a particular work was preserved, what works were forbidden or destroyed, and why the views were limited. From their modern history courses, students should know about genocide, propaganda, fascism, communism. From their own neighborhoods and families they may have learned racist and sexist values fostered by, perpetuated by, and reflected in all art forms. These experiences and values should be discussed. We should strive to understand what the artists and other people of the past did to survive, to create, and how their environments affected their perceptions and their work. We must be on guard for propaganda, dogma, and all the "isms" in the history books we read, for such things are as old as history and art. Even works that have survived can be overlooked by historians and critics who cannot think for themselves. Equipped with the proper vocabulary, analytical skills, and openmindedness, students should be able to think for themselves and to grow through their encounters with the arts. To let them accomplish this, teachers should encourage students to take advantage of opportunities to examine many kinds of art and to develop their own tastes freely.

There are too many examples of the lack of artistic and human freedom. In China during the Cultural Revolution, Beethoven's music was forbidden because it was foreign and elitist; in the United States at the same time (the late 1960s), a Polish-American acquaintance forbade the playing of polkas at her wedding because she felt they were "too ethnic." Part of developing aesthetic taste is learning when the fault lies in the art and when it lies in ourselves. After he became famous, Picasso paid for dinner, or anything else, by doodling on a paper because anything he did was worth thousands of dollars. In the 1970s a painter was praised for her murals for a firehouse wall in Cambridge (Massachusetts), while another painter was fined for "defacing" a wall in a neighboring city. Folk dancers were prohibited by Franco's regime from performing their regional dances. The works of Mendelssohn were banned by the Third Reich because the composer was a Jew. Jackson Pollock acquired Peggy Guggenheim as a patron by getting drunk and catching her attention at a party, while Chilean guitarist and songwriter Victor Jara had his hand smashed by the junta

20

to silence his protest songs. In Brazilian "snuff" films (throwbacks to the killing of slaves in the dramas of decadent ancient Rome), actresses were killed on screen; while Andy Warhol rented out actors and actresses to hang on walls at parties.

Whatever we teach—whether it is art or any other subject—we must teach our students not to accept anything just because it has always been that way. "Anything" includes not just governments that ban music or dancing, but also symphony programs, museum collections, television programs, theater bookings, the destruction of buildings. Students must learn how to separate the forms, functions, and contents of even the traditional works of art to decide what is being applauded and what is being left out and why. If they join traditionalists in their applause for Shakespeare or Beethoven or Rembrandt, their applause should come from genuine understanding and appreciation. Similarly, their rejection of works of art should come from educated appraisal, not from ignorance. We hope they will not see the arts as an unchanging decoration as colorless as black tie and tails, but rather as a constant evolution, sometimes even a revolution. We hope they will not ever join in censoring what they do not understand. We must encourage their curiosity and hope that they will encourage the expressions of all people, including those unlike themselves.

In the end, we come back to where we start: with ourselves and with these forms that please us because we like the way they look or sound or feel, and because we know our own living is enhanced enough to make us take a closer look. The arts then can bring young people to a better understanding of people in other places and other times, and ultimately to a better understanding of themselves.

Chapter 2

TEACHING STUDENTS HOW TO RESPOND TO THE ARTS: SUBJECT, FUNCTION, AND FORM

No matter how inspired by the arts and history we may be, we may find it difficult to spread our enthusiasm and to inspire curiosity in our students. In addition to motivating students, teachers must teach them how to respond to works of art. A curriculum should impose an order that will help students find patterns in the categories and chronologies of the humanities without sacrificing their own emotional, aesthetic, and intellectual responses to each work they encounter.

By viewing history as a pattern, as a series of interrelated cycles repeated in a variety of ways, we help to prepare students for new experiences and equip them to understand the past and the present and to be ready for the future. If history were merely the rote listing of chronological events, it would not qualify as one of the humanities. Thus, to become acquainted with the themes and issues of past, present, and future, students must be taught to see relationships, to think critically, to see how one thing is like or unlike another. From comparisons like these, students may come to viable conclusions and decisions. In mathematics and science they are taught to analyze and compare as part of deductive reasoning. This awareness of similarities and differences is also the essence of literature and other arts through metaphor, allegory, and symbolism. Finding relationships, then, is the essence of the study of humanities as well as the guiding principle for curriculum decisions in the humanities—relationships between music and art, literature and religion, ritual and dance, architecture and culture, religion and politics.

The separation of works of art into three aspects—subject matter, function, and form—helps students to respond, to make connections, to evaluate and analyze the arts on their own, to move from narrowness and subjectivity to viewpoints that are informed and objective.

SUBJECT

Subject matter is what the work of art represents, shows, tells about. In Leonardo's *Last Supper* the subject matter is Jesus and the disciples at the last supper, the seder held the night before he died. More specifically, it is the moment when they ask, "Is it I, Lord?" after he has told them that one of them would betray him. In a novel or play, the subject is the plot, the story, or more concisely, the summary of that story. In *King Lear* it could be stated as a king's abdicating his throne, disowning one daughter, dividing his kingdom between his two other daughters, and finally realizing his folly and lack of understanding of his daughters and himself. In *The Discus Thrower* the subject matter is an athlete about to throw the discus. In less clearly representational art forms, like instrumental music, the subject could be said to be a musical theme, a sequence of notes. In modern dance the subject is also less likely to be a story and more likely to be an abstract shape or motion, a dance motif. Abstract art and forms like jazz also make this first step of identifying subject matter more confusing and difficult, but no less exciting, than when it is clearly defined.

The student can choose a subject matter (for example, love), and then choose a medium (for example, vocal music), to find several treatments of that subject (for example, a native American love or courting song, a Renaissance madrigal, a baroque aria or duet, a folk song, a rock song). This activity can lead to a closer look at the various cultures represented and their views and customs concerning love, or it could lead to considerations of function and form (see below).

The student can consider the subject of *King Lear*, a father and his family, and relate that work to other plays about fathers and families—*Death of a Salesman,* for example, or *Oedipus*—and then to a consideration of these three different societies and their views of kingship or of family roles: Renaissance England, postwar America, and classical Athens. The subject matter is an excellent vehicle for drawing comparisons not only among works of art but also with the student's own feelings and experiences. For example,

23

students can write personal essays or even letters about their own fathers, their own families.

FUNCTION

Next, the question of function may occur to the student observer. In the case of the love songs, the student can try to find out when the song might be sung, by whom, to whom, and on what occasion. In every case these considerations of function will lead to an examination of the form since the form is so often dictated by the function. Is the song spontaneous or ritualistic, emotional or intellectual, public or private? Is it composed in a traditional way? How does all of this affect the form? Is it monophonic, polyphonic, modal, tonal? As a result of this exercise, mating or courting rituals may be researched; various musical forms can also be examined and, if possible, performed.

Similar questions about function can be asked about *The Last Supper* or *King Lear* or *Oedipus* or *The Discus Thrower*—their relationship to ritual, tradition, public or private expression, patronage. Some answers can be found through research, others through intuition. Aristotle helps students answer questions about subject, form, and function in his *Poetics*. Research materials as diverse as newspaper clippings and archaeologists' findings will also help with the study of function. To contrast the functions of war monuments, for instance, students can go from ancient religions and traditional art history books to accounts of the controversies that attended the design and competition for the Vietnam War Memorial in Washington. Such political, aesthetic, and cultural considerations add a focus that helps students approach questions of form—why or how the artist may have decided to tell his/her story—and decide the appropriateness and success of a particular work.

FORM

Moving from function to form, observing the work as if from a distance, students can consider what they know about the subject and the function and how these have affected the form. For example, the form of the play *Oedipus* is derived from ritual that honors the gods and is designed to recreate a painful event that will

24

cause catharsis in the audience. Thus it consists of the reenactment of myth and the use of formal choral poetry in a design that builds to a climax, a moment of awareness and crisis, pain and truth. Knowing this, students may begin to trace these parts in the play. Knowing the public function of Greek drama also will help. Likewise, a general understanding of the classical sense of proportion will help students appreciate *The Discus Thrower* or *The Parthenon* or the structure of Shakespeare's plays or the sonata-allegro form of a Mozart symphony. Knowing about Renaissance perspective and admiration of classical balance will help them see more readily the positioning of Jesus and the disciples in *The Last Supper*—that is, in four groups of three, six on either side of Jesus, who is in the center. This knowledge will help them see the significance of later works that intentionally do not employ classical or Renaissance traditions.

The most aesthetic activity of the three areas, the study of form, is also the most difficult and perhaps the most rewarding. Students are often amazed to find out how much English poetry is written in heroic couplet and blank verse, yet flows so smoothly that the untrained ear or eye might not hear or see how it was put together. They can feel this sense of discovery once their eyes and ears are trained. But an orderly analysis requires systematic steps without which many students will feel lost. To examine the form, three questions are essential: (1) How does the artist create order in this work (the order out of the chaos that nature presents all of us, artists or not)? (2) How does the artist unify the work? and (3) What kinds of contrast propel the work, make it move and come to a life of its own?

The first question, about order, is basic. The shaping of clay by the artist's hands or of marble by the artist's chisel or of rhythms and melodies and harmonies by the composer must happen first. But what thoughts and plans and experiences preceded the creating? Students may want to know about the artist's environment and the artist's life.

In each scene of *King Lear*, or any other play, the student can look for unity—by characters involved in the same scene; by motifs, imagery, allusions, metaphors, and situations; by themes. Or the student can notice how contrast is used by Shakespeare and every other writer—contrast of characters (good and bad, male and female, king and fool, romantic and realist), contrast of scenes (indoors, outdoors, loud, quiet, crowded, spare, about battles, about love, natural, supernatural), contrast of language (king and drunken porter, soliloquy and dialogue).

Even a work of art whose subject and function are unknown can evoke imaginative responses in students. If the art teacher shows a slide of *The Venus of Willendorf* (an ancient primitive form whose title *Venus* is a guess and *Willendorf* a reference to the place it was found), students can discuss what they think the subject and function were. They might suggest a religious or ritualistic function for such an object, based on their study of primitive societies. The *Venus* might evoke a discussion about the place of women in religion, in mythology, in various cultures. Such a mysterious yet evocative form will stay with them as they discuss sculpture as well as the portrayal of women in the arts through history.

Several more questions concerning order, unity, and contrast might be asked about form.

Order

Why does the novelist or playwright choose one particular month in the main character's life to focus on? Why does the painter show just so much of the room or the beach? Why does the sculptor sculpt just the hands of a person? Why does the story begin in the middle of the event? Why does it end at that moment in the characters' lives? Why does Homer focus on just a few events in the Trojan War in *The Iliad*? The same question can be asked of Euripides' *Trojan Women*. Answers to these questions are not always simple or self-evident, but discussions should get at the ways artists decide about what they want to show and how they go about it. Artists' choices of how they order their works are related to their views of the world, the event, the people, their philosophy, the points they wish to make about their subject.

Unity

In what ways does the artist unify the work? Does a certain color unify a painting, apart from the unity the subject matter gives it? Does a geometric shape unify a painting or sculpture? In *The Discus Thrower* the discus shape or circle unifies the sculpture. It is

26

both a representation of the athlete about to throw the discus and a study of circles—the discus, the athlete's head, the rounded arms. The student can see how the subject and form can come together in successful art. The shape of the discus may have inspired the sculptor to treat the subject in this particular, ingenious way that gives it added interest and life.

In a difficult novel like Faulkner's *As I Lay Dying*, the mother's dying and death are the unifying device because all the narrator's utterances are a result of these events, and the journey to bury her is the motif that brings all the parts together.

In music, the unifying device is rhythm or a set of variations or development of the same themes. Or is it the key that unifies the movement? In architecture, it is a motif like the arch or the column. Even in the Bible, in the Joseph story in Genesis, another kind of motif, a literary motif, a recurring element in the plot, unifies the work. There are three such motifs in the Joseph story: the dream motif, the death-and-resurrection (or imprisonment-escape) motif, and the change-of-clothes motif, all within the archetypal journey-of-a-hero frame. Such analysis of unifying elements helps the student differentiate a simple religious story from the great art that it is. *Motif* is one of the most important words in the study of the arts because every art form has its own type: plot, musical theme, visual pattern, choreographic pattern, structural pattern.

Contrast

Likewise every work of art employs contrast. The student is used to this in literature: protagonist versus antagonist, narration versus conversation. Sometimes the contrast is obvious, but it provides the emotional highs in music: from forte to piano, solo to chorus, adagio to allegro, solo to full orchestra. The same is true of the general forms of dance. In painting and photography the most obvious contrast is dark versus light.

IMPLEMENTATION

Though most students have studied novels closely, approaching a novel by considering order, unity, and contrast can emphasize the similarities between novelists and other artists and the choices a novelist must make in creating his/her art form. Kurt Vonnegut's *Slaughterhouse Five,* for example, lends itself to a discussion of the novelist making choices about subject, form, and function because in his first chapter he discusses these choices. The chaos that he seeks to make order from is World War II and his own memories of it and beyond—war, materialism, and mortality. Finding themes and motifs in the world is a creating of order. Discussing the function of such a novel, the student can see how the writer, or any artist, creates to make a point to others but also to express himself, to come to terms with various aspects of personal and universal experience.

The element of time unifies the novel in its science-fiction-like fragmented switches from past to present to future. The main character, Billy Pilgrim, who has "come unstuck in time," also unifies it, and through him Vonnegut deals with World War II, with the materialism of American life in the late sixties, and with the fantastic element of extraterrestrial and eternal life.

The switches in time and place (wartime Dresden, upstate New York at various times in Billy's life, and the planet of Tralfamadore) also provide contrast in the novel. This fragmentary device— of sudden switches—is a characteristic of Vonnegut's style in many novels. Any of the categories—subject (war, mortality, materialism), form (fragment, time-switches, intrusive narrator), or function (satire, humor, coming to terms with life, criticizing life)— can lead students from this novel to other works of art that (1) deal with the same subjects, (2) use similar forms and narrative devices, and (3) criticize the ways of the world. A simple question like "What other work of art does this novel remind you of?" can lead to revelations about art forms, subjects, topics, and themes.

Slaughterhouse Five is likely to remind students who have sampled many works of art from many periods of several works about war (*The Iliad, The Trojan Women, The Red Badge of Courage, Candide, All Quiet on the Western Front, Guernica,* various war monuments and sculptures from primitive to modern, protest and ironic poetry), specifically about World War II and about mortality and materialism. Then they may find other aspects within a few of these works to compare for more insight. The form might remind students of other fragmented forms (T. S. Eliot's "Love Song of J. Alfred Prufrock" and "The Wasteland," cubist paintings, even jazz), intrusive narrators (Fielding, Cervantes, Thackeray), and satires *(Gulliver's Travels, Candide* again). The discussion can lead in many different directions about art, culture, and ideas.

One student made such connections between the powerful Czech film *Shop on Main Street* (about a Jewish shop owner in Nazi-controlled Czechoslovakia) and *Slaughterhouse Five.* Both are about World War II, both employ dreams and fantasy as escapes from and contrasts to reality, both use humor and satire and irony, both have Chaplinesque main characters (Tono Britko in the film, Billy Pilgrim in the novel). The student's essay contained observations about the war, the victims, the guilty, the artistic tones and styles of the film and the novel.

Another student who had studied Picasso's *Guernica* kept seeing it again as he read *Candide.* The visual images of human suffering in *Guernica* kept recurring as he read of the human cruelty and suffering in *Candide* and compared the wars and the styles of the two artists. A third student had a similar experience when he read Jerry Kosinski's *The Painted Bird,* a grotesque episodic novel about a young Polish boy during World War II.

The subject-form-function process can be instructive even when the subject is as mundane as a nearby shopping mall, which leads the student to consider the issue of public architecture and the relationship between the arts and commerce and community.

Finally, a close look at one work may facilitate an understanding of a similar yet more inscrutable or difficult work for some students. Jazz or cubism can be bewildering, but literature can help students enter the world of fragmented, broken images and motifs in music and the visual arts. A "fragment" poem by T. S. Eliot can help them see that much of modern art is like Eliot's view of a "magic lantern" that throws the meaning "in patterns on a screen" (from "The Love Song of J. Alfred Prufrock"); the viewer must do the unifying of all the parts before making a final judgment about the meaning of the work or its success or failure. For other students, the poem or story may be unclear until a painting or a piece of music of a similar style is presented to them.

Chapter 3

A CASE STUDY

This chapter is based on the work of four teachers at Needham High School (Massachusetts) who have been teaching an interdisciplinary humanities course for high school seniors for two years. It is hoped that the description of their experience in planning and teaching the class will help other teachers.

STARTING A HUMANITIES COURSE

Before an interdisciplinary humanities course can become a reality, a group of teachers must break down the barriers that, even in the friendliest of schools, separate departments and compartmentalize learning. After the initial breakthrough is made, ongoing cooperation among the teachers of the humanities course can encourage cooperation, team teaching, and sharing of staff expertise throughout the school. Music and art departments especially tend to be isolated and can offer much to increase student involvement and interest in English, social studies, language, and even science and physical education classes. In large schools, before teachers can meet to discuss these options, there must be an opportunity for them to get to know each other.

Well in advance of scheduling or listing courses in the following year's program of studies, a full year or more before the course is to start, teachers involved must begin to meet. Directors must agree about staffing and put their trust in the teachers to write the trial curriculum. After the student signup, the teachers, directors, principal, and other administrators must agree on teacher assignments.

Evaluation of such a program will be complicated. Only the teachers can know just how time-consuming preparation and grading can be. Directors must become familiar enough to know how much time will be required for the course to be successful.

They (the directors), as well as other administrators and teachers, should be invited to visit the class and to join in some of team's meetings. If administrators understand the course and its scheduling, they should support those aspects of the course that require unusual, creative, and sometimes more expensive scheduling and staffing in order to keep the program multifaceted and rich. Given support and freedom, the teachers can improve the course through their own ongoing evaluation of one another's teaching. Finally, teachers and administrators can evaluate the course by viewing students' art, performances, reading projects, essays, and the students' own written evaluations.

Team teaching inevitably involves trial and error. Teachers must consider all subject areas involved—music, art, English, and social studies in our case—not just their own area. Also, they must be made comfortable enough to ask for more time and flexible enough to allow more time for each other's presentations, when necessary. One teacher should serve as coordinator, preferably one with experience in a few areas. Lack of time is the major source of frustration; all teachers can be relieved to know that the course is intended only as an introduction to a vast amount of learning and pleasure. Each teacher can expect to meet the class alone at least once a week, with joint lectures and presentations taking place at least once a week as well, for cohesiveness and variety. The English teacher, especially, will be frustrated when given only a few classes to focus on material that in a standard English course might take weeks to cover.

Planning must be long-range yet flexible enough so that snow days or other schedule changes will not be catastrophic. Due dates for essays and reading assignments and quizzes should be set by the beginning of the term to assure that the four areas will come together and important materials be covered. Schedules given to students should include due dates since there is less opportunity to remind students of approaching deadlines for other teachers. In other words, when more than one teacher is assigning homework, all teachers must keep track to set realistic and fair deadlines. Looseleaf notebooks might be required to encourage orderly notes and handouts from four different teachers. Students may complain about the initial complexity, but for the most part they will begin to feel that they are more independent and also better prepared for college.

Facilities

A creative staff can teach in any classroom, but a school with adequate music and art rooms has adequate facilities for a humanities course. In our case, we relied almost exclusively on what was in place: (1) a large chorus room with piano; (2) a band room with tiers for large class meetings, newly equipped with two pull-down screens for slides and films and two video screens provided by the audiovisual department when needed; (3) art facilities for pottery, sculpture, drawing, and photography; and (4) two classrooms, one for literature and one for history. Luckily, the two classrooms were at the end of the English and social studies corridors near the same set of stairs and ramps that lead to both music and art suites. Guest speakers and student performers used the band room. Physical education teachers rearranged their schedules to allow a folk dancer to hold classes in one of the gyms. If the course enrollment is small, however, one classroom with adequate audiovisual equipment might be enough. On the other hand, a large enrollment may make it necessary for three or four teachers to be scheduled into such a course. Allowing for team teaching, though, should be enough reason to modify teacher-student ratio requirements for the good of both teachers and students. With creative scheduling, more types of activities and better use of teacher expertise are possible.

ORGANIZING A STRUCTURE: FINDING PATTERNS

Most textbooks and anthologies in humanities disciplines present chapters and units that read like a history book, in chronological order. A chapter on ancient Greece is followed by a chapter on Rome, followed soon by a chapter on medieval Europe. While some students no doubt see connections and make contrasts among these separate units, the chronological order will not help them see patterns and relationships that have existed and continue to exist through the history of the arts and cultures. High school humanities teachers should try to find an organizing principle that, while not abandoning chronology completely, establishes some unity and highlights patterns to help students see the connections between the arts and cultures of all times. Often there is not a noteworthy connection between works of art created within the same year; the more edifying comparison comes from relating works of similar content, form, function, and values from cultures separated by centuries and continents.

Every creative teacher can find a philosophical approach that helps structure the course. One that I have found useful stresses the similarities of art forms and characteristics of cultures that would not appear in the same chapter or unit using a simple chronological view. This approach recognizes a repeating yet evolutionary cycle in history, containing predictable patterns that can be simplified as four stages of culture (see Table 1). Students use the stages as tools for recognizing trends, for making connections, for comparing and understanding cultures, epochs, and—more specifically—religions, philosophies, and works of art. Recognizing a similarity to an earlier culture or work increases the student's understanding of each subsequent culture studied. The pattern is a spiral with a continuing building of concepts that use chronologically earlier examples within each of the four stages as the basis of more extensive explanations of later examples. These four stages are (1) Primitive Tribal, (2) Primitive/Hierarchical, (3) Democracy/Republic, and (4) Decadent/Imperialist. All the arts—primitive, classical, romantic, or modern—merely find their places in these repeating cycles. The following pages contain lists of characteristics of each of the four "culture types," with examples. When used as a tool for comparison, this general structure also enables students to find new insights into art forms and cultures on their own in future responses to human expressions in arts and politics, rather than just labeling and compartmentalizing the past. (Because students seem particularly enthusiastic about the heterogeneity of the course, care must be taken to offer options within each epoch or stage or unit so that students of various backgrounds and abilities can learn together and from one another and get to know one another's talents and opinions.)

Primitive/Tribal Stage

Characteristics: Shared values and beliefs of all members, defined roles, art/magic/science/religion practiced as one, often matriarchal.

33

Table 1. Four Stages of Culture

| Stage | Visual Arts | | |
	Painting	Sculpture	Architecture
1. Primitive/ Tribal	Sand painting Masks Graffiti Sidewalk art	Totem poles Venus of Willendorf	Teepee

2. Primitive/ Hierarchical	Illuminated
	  manuscripts
	Pyramid murals
	Chinese Cultural
	  Revolution
		In Pyramids
		Puritan gravestones
		Medieval sculpture
			Pyramids
			  Mayan
			  Aztec
			  Egyptian
			Knossos
			Cathedrals

3. Democracy/ Republic	daVinci Classical style	Michelangelo Donatello	Parthenon Pantheon Il Duomo Washington, D.C.
4. Decadent/ Imperialist	Baroque	Laocoon Bernini	St. Peter's Colosseum Nazi architecture

Table 1. Four Stages of Culture (Continued)

Literature		Performing Arts		Social Studies
Prose	Poetry	Drama	Music	
Myth Bible *Bhagavad Gita* *Lord of the Flies* *Things Fall Apart* *Siddhartha* Folk sermon	*Odyssey* *Beowulf*	Ritual Living theater Folk drama	Rap Native American Blues Chanting	Tribes Hare Krishnas Shakers Punk Various movements, cults
Puritan sermons *The Fixer*	Chaucer Dante	Miracle, Morality, Mystery plays	Gregorian chant	Mayans Feudalism Hero worship God-King Witch trials Inquisition Holy War Caste system Czarist Russia Chinese Cultural Revolution
Satire Hawthorne Swift Pope Voltaire	Sappho Sonnets Pope Johnson	Aeschylus Sophocles Euripides Shakespeare Arthur Miller	Madrigal Motet Polyphony Suite Mozart Haydn Sonata-Allegro form	Greece Rome Renaissance Early U.S. Republic Neoclassicism Capitalism
	Milton Donne	Late Roman plays		Hellenistic Age Roman decadence Baroque Age 1920s U.S. Pre-Nazi/Nazi Germany Isms Communism Fascism Socialism Capitalism

Later Types: Political, religious, and art movements; antiestablishment; belief in a new order: rejection of king, empire, imperialism, dictator, hierarchy; often a romantic style.

Examples: Native Americans, African tribes, ancient India, catacomb Christians, revolutionaries, cults, sects, dissenters, Puritans, Pilgrims, romantic poets, early Nazis, dadaists, hippies, feminists, antiwar groups, anti-nuke groups, 1960s folk revival, Hare Krishnas, Black Muslims, communes, monasteries.

Sample Activities

The teacher or student can gather examples of works of art, statements of belief, first-person accounts, interviews with members of cults or movements, to show connections between tribal societies of the past and present-day groups identified as out of the mainstream and having characteristics associated with tribes, and people who identify themselves through a "tribe." Native American tribes can be studied through their myths, rituals, poetry, religion, use of art (from sand paintings to masks), social customs and roles. "Tribes" from other parts of the world, especially Africa, can be compared. This unit becomes more vital to students if actual representatives of groups (such as Native Americans) are invited to class to speak, perform, or be interviewed. Various aspects of their life and art can be studied in comparison with contemporary groups or with other periods of history—for example, costumes, masks, rites of passage, painting, the roles of shaman or magician or artist or priest or chief.

The social studies teacher might introduce primitive cultures and anthropology in this unit. Religious cults, sects, and communities are also tribal in nature and could be studied as a way of understanding this type of cultural phenomenon—for example, Hare Krishnas, Black Muslims, Shakers, cloistered monks and nuns (Christian or Buddhist), Moonies. Nineteenth-century romantics who rejected the mainstream also could be studied in relation to kindred spirits like hippies of the 1960s or people who choose communal life.

The art teacher might use primitive art forms to discuss rituals and beliefs and have students create their own art: sand paintings, pottery, masks, costumes, totems. Students might work on contemporary equivalents of these forms (such as sidewalk art, murals, graffiti). The incentive for joining a modern-day tribe can be related to the arts, too, from dadaists and impressionists to mods and rockers and punks and beatniks of more recent decades. Students can compare statements of beliefs and values and accounts of lifestyles of these artists.

The literature and music teachers can work together on poetry and song and their relationships to primitive societies. Students should be able to compare their own subculture of adolescence to various themes and rituals in tribes. Storytelling and rap music and various creative exercises could be attempted—for example, drumming, chanting, setting myths to music, creating myths and tales. With some effort students should be able to find people who belong to subcultures and invite them to speak or to be interviewed. The relationship between politics and the arts may also be examined. Those who choose a tribal or primitive style are likely to choose direct protest rather than a more sophisticated type of satire to express opposition to mainstream values. The 1960s folk revival is a rich area of study because it contains such a variety of forms associated with the primitive: folk music, dance, living theater, crafts, clothing, communal living, herbal or folk medicine, interest in native American arts. Holistic medicine and the use of crystals and other phenomena associated with matriarchal religions are more recent manifestations of the primitive that student researchers might investigate.

The basic questions in the humanities about life, creation, death, and every other human concern, first answered in myths and rituals, can serve as an introduction to music, literature, poetry, drama, and dance. The literature teacher might focus on non-Western traditions, myths, and religions in comparison with Western traditions, exploring areas such as mythology and the Bible, Judaism and Christianity. Genesis should be compared with the myths of other ancient peoples, for example. Further, contemporary issues and viewpoints become clearer when students consider differences between matriarchal and patriarchal societies. Focusing on a few Greek myths, American Indian poems and myths, and stories from Genesis, students may make comparisons in terms of values that remain in conflict today. For example, matriarchal concerns include the environment (Greenpeace, antinuclear groups), peace (antiwar groups), homelessness; while patriarchal concerns include defense buildup, patriotism, free enterprise.

The English teacher should choose literature that would prompt students to ask questions about primitive people and their responses to their environment, their humanity, the natural and the supernatural. In addition, students can choose more ancient readings to help characterize and contrast ancient forms, religions, and subjects: other books from the *Old Testament,* the *Bhagavad Gita, Tao Te Ching,* an epic (*The Iliad* or *The Odyssey* or *The Aeneid* or *Beowulf*). Modern works with themes related to primitive cultures and religions can also be read both for contrast and for showing the continuing relevance of these themes: *Lord of the Flies, Things Fall Apart, Siddhartha, J.B.* Thus in the first term each student should read at least two modern novels plus a collection of myths, folktales, or stories from the Bible, epic poetry, and at least one Greek play during the classical unit.

The literature and social studies teachers might show clashes of cultures through literature and history. These conflicts become more understandable when students have compared native American and other ancient cultures with those of Salem Puritans, for example.

Students' tendency to identify with members of tribes and groups can be quite strong. Those who cannot relate to ancient or distant tribes might relate to the many contemporary subcultures, cults, and movements. A discussion of the beliefs and rituals of such movements can lead students to see connections between the earliest and simplest societies and groups that break away from or are excluded from the mainstream. The political implications of the arts and the manner in which history is written should be made clear so that no art form is studied in a vacuum because none exists in a vacuum. Students' attitudes about their own and others' religions, ceremonies, dances, music, clothing should be seen as important and worth expressing. Many differences of opinion and values are bound to be expressed; as a result students will see the variety of styles at a given time and place in history—their own time and place. Indeed, the class may consist of teen-aged feminists, chauvinists, atheists, agnostics, traditionalists, revolutionaries, conservatives, liberals, and romantics. The more discussion about taste and reasons for taste that students have among themselves, the more receptive they will be to reading about the tastes of other times and cultures. (In this unit a folk dancer related dance to other primitive art forms and societies and taught students a few dances, while an artist and anthropologist gave presentations on Aztec and Polynesian art.)

Primitive / Hierarchical Stage

Characteristics: Unified by conquest or need for food and land; populous; class structure, including slavery; hierarchy and religion connected; theocracy; focus on supernatural, death, afterlife; leader often deified; written laws; rigidity; technical and scientific development, but not social; change comes very slowly or not at all; patriarchal.

Examples: Egyptians, Minoans, Mayans, Aztecs, caste system of India, medieval Europe, Salem witch-trial era, pre-Revolutionary France, Czarist Russia, Third Reich, Stalinist Russia, Cultural Revolution in the People's Republic of China, South Africa, Iran today, Haiti.

Sample Activities:

To demonstrate the difference between stages one and two, after students read Exodus and its accounts of the pharaoh's treatment of the Jews, they should be shown the monumental wonders of the pyramids and all the great art they contain. Then they will see the contrast between the simple stories of a tribe (the Israelites) and the art of a culture the employs slave labor and deifies its leader. Also, the Gospel of Matthew and Pier Paolo Pasolini's primitive 1966 cinema-verité-style film version of the Gospel can serve as a bridge from the ancient world to the middle ages. The history teacher can assign a few students to study each of the cultures listed above. Then small groups could compare their findings with those of the other groups—for example, Egyptian, Mayan, Russian (under the Czar, then under Stalin), Chinese, South African laws, legal systems, and social stratifications, with their rationales. The importance of the religious or political philosophy in the laws and the arts might also be researched. Another activity could focus on the leaders of these societies, through biography or as part of a lesson on hero-worship, charisma, and deification: pharaoh, medieval king, czar, Hitler, Mussolini (or save them for Stage 4), Stalin, Mao, the Ayatollah, the Japanese emperor, the Pope. Comparison with other types of heroes and leaders might help to distinguish this stage from others (native American chiefs, Che Guevara, George Washington, Moses).

Students should be able to find documents and speeches as well as art forms from cultures of many epochs to see how similar these seemingly dissimilar cultures can be: accounts from Salem witch trials; sermons from Salem or from medieval Europe; accounts of the Crusades or of the tortures of the Inquisition or of the Ayatollah's Holy War against Iraq; descriptions of the caste system of India and the racial policies of South Africa, and of the Red Guard's purges during the Cultural Revolution in China. If the Holocaust is not to be studied separately, it can be done effectively in the context of this unit. Propaganda should be introduced with this second stage, recognizing that the power of monumental art, like that of mass media arts, is extremely persuasive. Second-stage societies should be studied as a warning of the kind of techniques and art forms a democracy must avoid or at least be wary of.

The art teacher might present exemplary works of art from the preceding list of cultures (e.g., the pyramids of Egyptians, Mayans, and Aztecs; and the medieval cathedrals) and have students compare their forms, functions, contents, related rituals, myths. Other works could include medieval European and seventeenth-century Salem sculptures and gravestones; uniforms and clothing of various ranks in Egypt, India, medieval Europe, and Czarist Russia. One student related medieval Europe to China during the Cultural Revolution, focusing on dogma and the highly stylized paintings and illuminations that depict workers or peasants in both societies. She considered questions such as, What is this painting about? What do you think its function was? How are these people shown? Are they realistic? Such questions will make both medieval Europe and the Chinese Cultural Revolution clearer to students.

Another student chose the treatment of death and the afterlife in reliefs and rituals of ancient Egypt, contemporary Haiti, and seventeenth-century Massachusetts. He examined tomb reliefs in books and at the Museum of Fine Arts in Boston, accounts of voodoo rituals in books, Puritan gravestones in local cemeteries, and sermons in books.

Much medieval art shows that the second stage is not a dead end but rather part of an evolutionary process in which great artists and thinkers find ways within the old forms and philosophies to create new ones, and within the old moral code to take what was best.

They examine life in a human, fair, and wise manner, presenting the truth in a beautiful way that outlives the limits of the time. That is why great art often comes from narrowing and suffocating periods. Great artists were meant for all time. By putting the arts into perspective with the times, students are able to understand and appreciate great artists and their work much more than if they study the art alone. Here, too, the literature teacher might assign Chaucer's *Canterbury Tales* and Dante's *Inferno*, brilliant examples of writing, which are also among the best resources for insight into the foibles and weaknesses of human nature as well as the ideals and beliefs of that time.

Besides the study of forms of the arts and culture, the humanities are an examination of ideas and of as many perspectives on life as possible. Such study will result in discussions on religion, morality, and politics. For example, a modern ironic novel like *The Fixer* evoked strong feelings about antisemitism in czarist Russia and in medieval Europe in one student. She felt so oppressed by the overwhelming Christian focus of the art being studied in class that she did not want to enter the room when a medieval church atmosphere was being simulated with slides, incense, candles, and Gregorian chant. Reading the novel had given her a feeling that strengthened her own Jewish identity but may also have made her see anything Christian as pro-Christian and, by implication, against other religions. Other students found the novel anti-Russian, at least anti-Russian-Christian. These reactions led to expressions of deep feeling and discussions about the ways majority and minority students perceive art, religion, and their connections to politics. Some students will want to talk about views of women, foreigners, and the poor, about castes and racism; they will also see that many people in the world today are still living in this second stage.

The performing arts teacher might introduce Gregorian chant, comparing it with ancient Jewish ritual and then focusing on the connections between ritual and drama. And medieval morality plays can be related to revolutionary works in Iran and China (drama and dance).

Democracy/Republic Stage (Classical)

Characteristics: Society as a meeting of citizens; equality, though slavery and inequalities exist; public art; focus on government, on a better life, on the individual, not on death or the afterlife; philosophy and the arts replace religion and superstition; freedom and curiosity in arts allowed; criticism, satire, protest; inward examination, refinement; classical style.

Examples: The Age of Pericles (Golden Age), early days of Rome, early American republic, Renaissance in Europe, neoclassical era (eighteenth century).

Sample Activities

The transition to the third stage turns our attention toward reality, toward this world, away from one uniform view, diversity, curiosity, to the individual and quite literally, in painting, from two dimensions to three. Human beings are no longer two-dimensional types, good or evil, king or peasant, pharaoh or slave, saved or damned, Black or white, no longer defined merely by rank or uniform.

These more or less democratic cultures, known for their classical art, openness, experimentation, may seem like sudden miracles, breaths of fresh air. But it is the continuing story of culture that must be emphasized. Gradually some people were enlightened, through curiosity and creativity, to help their cultures come out of the uniforms and the darkness to examine reality and to assert their individuality. In more open atmospheres, art and criticism flourished. Primitive rituals evolved into drama that became more and more realistic, that cleansed the audience and made them more aware. Characters of myth and legend were brought to life, albeit in very formal style behind masks, but examined, made real, made human. Sculpture and painting were made more lifelike, perhaps not looking like the average person, but of this earth. A barbarian age was ended. Europeans in the Renaissance believed the same was true: in their opinion the Middle Ages were a Gothic or barbarian time, and it was time to return to classical forms, to focus on people not for religion's sake but to examine what it was like to live in this world. The search for truth and reason was as great in the new American republic, though this time it was achieved by force since England's medieval control over the colonies would not end gradually. It was a revolution that asked for reason. It should be no surprise to students that the new capital of Washington was built in neoclassical style. (The focus on Europe rather than on America for seventeenth and eighteenth century arts presupposes a strong course in American literature [and history] in the junior year. Comparisons are made of the Puritans and American philosophers and revolutionaries.)

The third stage is one of great drama because it is a period of concern for the place of human beings in society, in the world, in the community. It is time of open examination of difficulties public and private, from the Greek plays about kingship, war, personal love and suffering, and family relationships *(Oedipus, The Trojan Women, Medea, Hippolytus, Agamemnon, Electra)* to Shakespeare's plays about the same difficulties *(Macbeth, Hamlet, King Lear)*. In this climate of appreciation and excitement about the arts, subject matter and form come together elegantly and flawlessly. Consider daVinci's paintings, Michelangelo's sculptures, Shakespeare's sonnets, Palestrina's madrigals. In this stage, too, begin free enterprise, capitalism, the middle class as a viable group, the modern age, the end of superstition. Here begin the Reformation, the shaking off of the old, diversity, artists expressing their own views. This is an opportunity for the English teacher to teach Shakespeare in a new way, comparing his subject matter, forms, and style with those of Renaissance artists of other media. In his plays can be found an examination of human nature, of the classical world, of the medieval world, in the most elegant and beautiful language ever written, the ultimate literary marriage of meaning and form.

Skeptical and sensitive students will look beyond the glowing lights of Shakespeare and other Renaissance masters to notice antisemitism and other negative aspects of the new capitalism—colonialism, the destruction of primitive societies in America and Africa, the theft of their riches, the enslavement of their people, the seeds of future hierarchical totalitarianism, just as earlier cultures had contained the seeds of democracy. The excitement of these third-stage cultures, however, lies in the idealism that believes anything is possible through discovery, experimentation, examination; that other bright people will join in these searches without fear. Discovery, experimentation, and examination cannot take place in the midst of witch-hunts and inquisitions. There is a purity of spirit, more like that of stage one than any other, a spirit seeking truth and beauty through self-examination of the individual and of the society. In such an atmosphere, when individuals or governments act foolishly or extravagantly, the artists and critics examine the behavior and respond.

In such relatively healthy societies, satire is not only born but encouraged. Satyr plays originated in classical Athens; the great age of satire was a neoclassical era, the eighteenth century. Satire continues to flourish in societies that are open and democratic. For outside reading, students might choose from a list of seventeenth, eighteenth, and nineteenth century novels to prepare for quizzes and discussions of themes, subjects, narrative voice, and style and comparisons with historical events and elements in other media of the time: *Don Quixote, Moll Flanders, Joseph Andrews, Candide, Gulliver's Travels, Jane Eyre, Wuthering Heights, A Tale of Two Cities, Alice in Wonderland, Silas Marner,* and *Crime and Punishment.*

Protest, a simpler, more direct, and perhaps more naive form of satire, also flourishes in open societies and demonstrates again the kinship between first- and third-stage cultures. When the once-pure Athenian government started to strut around Greece and to wage war on other cities, beginning its march toward the Hellenistic age and its own transition to a stage-four culture, a great artist was troubled. To protest the government's warmongering, Euripides wrote *The Trojan Women.* It was fitting—and not surprising to the student who knows the meaning of stage four—that Euripides should focus on the women's role and on suffering in a war that otherwise was the subject of epics that glorified its heroes. Euripides was reminding his audience of the matriarchal aspect of society and of human nature, an aspect patriarchal wars attempt to wipe out. It had been a stage-two culture, Mycenae and related states, that waged war on Troy and destroyed its women. It was a stage-three artist who saw the evil of war and wanted to warn his society not to fall away any further from the civilization it had achieved. In fact, all the great classical Athenian playwrights took close, serious, realistic looks at the characters who had been portrayed romantically in earlier hero myths.

Similarly, Renaissance artists like Shakespeare took close looks at the excesses of medieval monarchies like those of Macbeth, Hamlet, and Lear and used them to present a stage-three view of humans and society. Similarly, too, Hawthorne looks back on a stage-two culture in *The Scarlet Letter, Young Goodman Brown,* and *The House of the Seven Gables.* From a twentieth-century

44

stage-three culture Arthur Miller examines the same stage-two culture, Salem, in *The Crucible*. Perhaps it is the fear, like Miller's, that our stage-three culture is corrupt and taking on characteristics more appropriate to stages two or four, that impresses artists to look back at previous cultures and to use them as settings for their works. In some cases, of course, it is only sentimentality or nostalgic romanticism that turns the artist back in time.

In addition to the study of previous topics such as the Reformation, capitalism, and other political, religious, and economic considerations, the history teacher can focus on philosophers (Socrates, Plato, Thomas More, Machiavelli, Hobbes, Locke, Rousseau), descriptions of various societies (Greece, Rome, Renaissance Italy, eighteenth-century England or France), forms of government, new freedoms and reforms in these epochs. And students can enjoy biographies of many colorful people from these times (Luther, Henry VIII).

The art teacher can focus on (1) classical style in sculpture, relief, painting, and architecture; (2) the ideals that made later societies look back to the classical forms for inspiration; (3) new concerns about realism and nature that also arise in these stage-three societies (perspective, foreshortening, mimesis, and naturalism). Architecture studies would also be of interest to students: comparisons of specific buildings (the Parthenon, the Pantheon, Il Duomo, the Jefferson Memorial), as well as of the general architecture of cities (Athens and Washington, New York and Rome, London and Boston).

The literature teacher's primary focus would be drama (classical Athenian and Shakespearean) because of the importance of public art at these times and the greatness of the plays. He/She can also include the episodic novel, satire (Swift, Pope, Voltaire), and didactic, philosophical poetry (Pope, Johnson).

The music teacher can present music's equivalent of the flowering of Renaissance religious, mythological, and secular paintings and techniques like perspective: new settings of the Mass, madrigals, motets, other contrapuntal, polyphonic music. He/She can also show how Western music depends on theories from classical Greece (Pythagoras) and how eighteenth-century composers like Mozart and Haydn use classical aesthetic principles in the sonata-allegro form and generally in their refined, logical, orderly, neo-classical styles.

Decadent/Imperialist Stage

Characteristics: Power, conquest, propaganda, sensationalism; emphasis on hierarchy, wealth versus slavery (extremes of class); militarism, leaders become dictators or gods; grandeur and size important; superstitions return; emphasis on quantity and glamour, not quality; spectacle; excess, not simplicity.

Examples: Hellenistic style; decadence in the Roman Empire; baroque period; Germany and the United States in the 1920s.

Sample Activities

Though evolution is the appropriate term for the transition from one stage to another, the change is obviously not always a positive one. At least since the seventeenth century, the diversity of cultures and beliefs in the world has added the complicating factor of revolution to the dynamics of history and of the humanities. Much of the seventeenth century might be considered a time of baroque art, but it is also the setting for a sudden break with tradition. In the case of the Pilgrims who left for America, it is a clean and lasting break. For those European societies that did not break so completely, a turn away from baroque excesses meant a return to many stage-three characteristics and to neoclassical style. But in other respects decadence and imperialism of one type or another helped to bring about the revolutions of the late eighteenth century. Ironically, it was the stage-three kind of openness in England and France that allowed for protest and satire and the kind of examination of governments that led to revolutions in both government and the arts.

Since 1800 most European and American societies have seemed to remain in various degrees of stages three and four, but various movements in the arts and in politics have been extreme and closer to the primitive spirit of stage one. For the past 200 years, revolutions have been toppling imperialist or decadent states in many parts of the world; revolutions in the arts have been equally frequent. Romanticism and its movements, ranging from social revolution to Victorian nostalgia to the end of the romantic era and the outbreak of World War I, should be studied in this stage three-four context. Poetry readings can begin with Burns, Blake, and the English romantic poets. Frequent comparisons and joint presentations can be made, relating romantic poetry to the American and French revolutions, to Beethoven's music, to naturalism in painting. Neoclassicism and romanticism can be contrasted. Students can be asked to choose a writer, a painter or sculptor, and a composer to compare and show similarities in subject matter, message, and function (Wordsworth, Millet, Courbet, Beethoven, Schumann; impressionism from Renoir to Debussy). A few nineteenth century plays can be read (Ibsen and Chekhov) to show the beginnings of modern drama and to relate them to primitive, medieval, classical, and Renaissance drama. Students can choose from a second list of turn-of-the-century novels to read during the term, including Thomas Hardy, Joseph Conrad, Oscar Wilde, D. H. Lawrence. A likely bridge from stage three to stage four is *All Quiet on the Western Front*.

During the study of stage four, the social studies teacher might present Crane Brinton's *Stages of Revolution*. Students can then use the formula to compare many periods and movements, including the Puritans of the seventeenth century, the French and Americans of the eighteenth, the Russians of the early twentieth, and turbulent periods like the 1960s. Students can also relate these periods and movements to the arts of the times, whether or not the arts are experiencing a revolution.

This classification is controversial in that Americans differ as to when a "democracy" can become "imperialistic." The British have also differed concerning their empire. Many of the characteristics listed above for stage four are also true of stage two cultures, but I have placed in stage four those that are the result of a stage-three culture that has become corrupted as it grew or changed, that has changed its emphasis from inward to outward display and conquest.

Stage four is especially rich for the history teacher as a time to examine "isms"—especially capitalism, socialism, communism, and fascism—and how they develop from stage-three societies. Students may pose hypotheses about the historical fact that governments that produced grand works of art also persecuted minorities, that excessive displays of wealth and ornamentation came at times of great poverty as well (the baroque age in Italy and France, the 1920s in the United States and Germany).

The art and music teachers can collaborate on the baroque period to show similarities in the emotional, repetitious, lively, theatrical styles of architecture (St. Peter's), painting (Rubens, Caravaggio), sculpture (Bernini), instrumental music (Vivaldi, Corelli), and vocal music (Handel, Purcell), as well as in the more complicated, introspective art forms (Bach, Rembrandt).

The art and literature teachers can collaborate with the history teacher to discuss sensationalism and decadence in Rome, in the Hellenistic period with regard to sculpture *(The Laocoon)*, drama (slaves killed on stage), emperor worship and gladiatorial combat, as well as minority persecution and underground societies (the catacombs of Rome, the Resistance during the Holocaust).

In the early twentieth century, after 100 years of various types of romanticism (most of them by then quite stodgy, counterrevolutionary, sentimental, nostalgic, and reactionary), artists like T. S. Eliot, Stravinsky, Picasso, and Gauguin rejected romanticism and turned to various forms of abstract art that are closer to primitive than to stages two or three. Of course, World War I helped put an end to the old tradition and the old romanticism. And long before that, the Civil War, the Industrial Revolution, Darwin, Marx, and a realism that photography might exemplify most symbolically had made it clear that the new world was to be a different and more confusing place. Together, the four teachers responsible for the humanities course can present and compare abstract art, cubism, jazz, existentialism, the absurd in drama, science fiction, satire and irony, and the mass media. Reading selections might include Beckett, Albee, Sartre, T. S. Eliot, Wallace Stevens, Yeats, Dylan Thomas, Marianne Moore, Levertov, Sexton, Plath. Outside reading options can include, in two assignments, (1) Joyce, Woolf, Faulkner, or Camus, and (2) Vonnegut, Orwell, Anthony Burgess, or Bradbury.

IMPLEMENTATION

A course that presents history through its arts and offers the tools to put all its scattered pieces together can make the student's world a less confusing place. The format and teacher strategies in this course depend on the styles and backgrounds of the teachers involved as well as their experience in working together and coordinating lessons. Teachers first present their material separately. Then each one leads a smaller group discussion based on the lecture and the homework or an in-class activity. At the end of this cycle of four lectures and four discussions, the four teachers get together with the class to discuss relationships in the materials. The tenth day of each of these ten-day cycles can be used for a guest lecture or performance or a field trip. Time should be allowed for performances—drama, dance, instrumental music, singing—and visits to museums, galleries, churches, and synagogues at the appropriate point in the schedule. These can be valuable, memorable experiences.

Within each class, material can be presented either inductively or deductively. For example, Renaissance paintings can be shown and discussed by students before the teacher describes the characteristics of Renaissance art, or the teacher can show the paintings after lecturing. Of course, the same is true of music, poetry, and drama. The history teacher might present a discussion topic for students to deal with before telling them how historical figures dealt with the situation.

As always, teachers have many options for making their subject approachable and exciting. Because the materials in this course are so rich and varied, students tend to be quite receptive. Teachers should not miss the opportunity to create classes that go beyond their perspective to inspire some sense of the wonder of all this history and art. They must avoid merely performing for or trying to entertain the class. Students should never be mere spectators. Moreover, any prolonged music listening or slide viewing or dramatic performance should come *after* students have learned about these forms. Nor should teachers, alone, in pairs, or all together, theorize or give personal opinions at too great a length without presenting material and examples as a way for students to become *actively involved* in a discussion.

Exposure to great art is one goal of this course, but without direction it is worth only a fraction of its worth with direction. Time is so valuable, however—with four teachers and thousands of years of history and arts vying for 150 hours in the school year—that only material that illustrates points, explains, sets standards, evokes thoughts and questions (specific or open-ended), or shows connections, and material that does not exclude the student should be used in class. For example, if music is played for 10 to 15 minutes, a text should be available and clear instructions given students as to what to listen for and what to relate it to. If slides are shown, unless a discussion or questions focus on individual slides, the viewing should lead to active student participation. In other words, students should know what to look or listen for. English teachers follow the same rules when dealing with difficult and rich yet potentially satisfying materials like Shakespeare's plays. Before an entire play, or even a single scene, is viewed, it is taken line by line to point out its structure, characterization, and meaning, and ultimately its beauty and power.

Beyond these separate analyses of representative works, the possibilities for combining materials for single classes are many and exciting. For example, the filmstrip *Baroque Art and Music* (1) effectively shows similarities between Rubens's frescoes and Bach's concerti, Vivaldi's sonatas and Bernini's sculpture and architecture, Rembrandt's etchings and Bach's Passion settings, Handel's arias and a host of baroque paintings. Teachers can conduct similar activities in class with the drama, sculpture, architecture, and music of primitive tribes, of classical Greece, of the middle ages and the Renaissance; or with twentieth-century artists such as T. S. Eliot, Picasso, and Stravinsky. Finally, teachers can encourage spontaneity and creativity by introducing an idea or topic or theme or subject and having students work on it in a variety of forms—for example, as a poem, a painting, a sculpture, an instrumental piece, a song, a scene or short story, a film. Such a project should be carried out at a point in the course when the topic will evoke such responses as liberty, justice, alienation, God, family, slavery, the future, existentialism, fascism. Then, surrounded by the works they have studied and the works they have created, students will know and feel that the arts and the humanities are theirs.

Chapter 4

STUDENT REACTIONS TO THE COURSE

Students representing most of the ability levels, backgrounds, and tastes in the senior class take this course, learning together and from one another. Though many socialize outside class, some clearly do not. Studious, introverted young people who take notes vociferously react to the comments of less academic, more "free-spirited" peers of many interests from punk to the Grateful Dead. The following pages describe some "types" of students to show what they have brought to the course, what they think about it, and what they seem to be getting from it.

Jennifer has never liked school, especially English, because she is a slow reader. She is shy, and she does not have many friends in the class. She has difficulty writing organized essays and understanding subtleties, but she struggles through the reading. She is enthusiastic about the chance to express herself about things other than literature, especially politics and religion. She seldom speaks out in class, but on a field trip to a modern Irish play, she talked about her grandfather's experiences in the Irish Republican Army. I allow her to rewrite essays to be sure they have clear theses, enough information, and conclusions. Jennifer told her English teacher from last year that this course means something to her.

Christine spent last year in a drug rehabilitation program. She has improved her attendance considerably and is very vocal in class about issues raised and about her enjoyment of the topics and activities. Her essays are completed on time and are frank about her own experiences and opinions related to cultural issues. She and her friends tend to sit in one corner of the band room during larger presentations, but they are attentive and participate. According to one of her friends, an intense young poet who would have been more at home in the late sixties than he is in the present, this group talks about issues raised in class while at one another's houses late into the night. Another friend, a boy definitely "beyond the fringe" of the high school who sees himself as an anarchist and is having trouble this year disciplining himself to get any schoolwork done, is taking the course for eight credits (double the usual amount) and is one of the most active participants in class discussions. Certainly his comments are original and cause many students to think about aspects of the arts and culture that they had not thought about before.

Two girls, also in this "fringe" group, both artistic and both with difficult family and personal situations, found the academic aspect of the work hard to keep up with and to organize. They had decided to drop the course and take the regular senior literature course. The art teacher in our team felt their talent in art and their sensitivity made them naturals for the humanities course. We both talked to them and convinced them to stay. Such encouragement is a positive aspect of a course that is team-taught. Despite the large number of students, 53 at that time, four teachers can give them personal attention when it is needed.

Many students have talent that can be developed and, in a few cases, discovered, in this course. Several bright students, with little background in photography or art history, decided to do photographic studies of Boston and other area locales based on architectural forms studied in class. The results, "Classical Boston" and "Gothic Boston," inspired classmates to try this type of project and motivated the students to consider photography as a hobby and history as a subject to elect in college. A few students have developed their satiric talents in stories, poems, and videotapes related to the periods and themes studied in the course, from modern-day suburban odysseys to interviews with pharaohs and Greek philosophers to parodies of romances, epics, and horror movies. (One videotape deals with fears of urban crime expressed by local people when the commuter train was brought back to our suburban town. Several artistic but decidedly nonacademic students worked on this tape, which was quite successful and applauded by their classmates.)

Many students with acting ability have acted in their own productions in retellings and parodies of the stories of Job, Antigone, Macbeth, and Romeo and Juliet.

The most independent and talented seniors are attracted to this course, and they have helped to make it extraordinary. They have created authentic teepees, classical columns, gilt mummies, mosaics, costumes for their plays as well as medieval and Egyptian costumes, dance and musical performances of traditional and original dances and music, and a great many original poems, short stories, and plays. One student musician rewrote or transcribed Renaissance lyre music for his six-string guitar and wrote an original version of a madrigal. Students have teamed up for these creative projects, helping each other to create things they might not have attempted alone.

Laura, a bright artist/musician/advanced placement English student, presented a 15-minute lecture on Celtic art with slides and other audiovisual aids. Besides allowing her to show her sense of humor as well as her intelligence and good taste, it appealed to all students because the entire class had been studying the Middle Ages together (unlike situations in which reports are unrelated to the material others have been studying).

Katrina has been studying sign language. She taught another student an interpretive signing of a Cat Stevens song ("Father and Son"). Their performance was like a dance. Students and teachers found it tremendously moving. The other student memorized one of Ophelia's scenes with her father and followed it by reciting an original poem or words Ophelia might have uttered after Polonius left the room.

Other students have composed rap songs, prepared various foods for the class from Greek to medieval English to homemade ice cream, and discussed religious beliefs and rituals covering several centuries.

In their choices of topics for essays and projects, students express themselves as artists, philosophers, theologians, drama critics, even city planners. One student, who had never been to a play, has been to four in a row. (We subscribed to a series, reserving 40 tickets for four different plays.)

Whatever level of creativity it touches, the course is a examination of human responses to history. David, who had viewed himself as an athlete and had never seen himself as academic or creative, has been researching areas like sports in ancient Greece, King Arthur, and other long-time interests. He says he has gotten the most out of being in a class with so many different types of students with so many interests unlike his own. One result is that David was encouraged to try some new experiences. Consequently, he tried out for the school musical and got the lead male role.

To meet the many diverse needs and interests of students, the team of teachers must experiment with scheduling continually. It is important to keep the course heterogeneous. The teachers need to determine interest in areas like creative and nonfiction writing, singing, acting, drawing, traveling to form groups of students to work with one another and one of the teachers in workshop settings. At least one teacher should be available to work with individuals and groups in remedial or accelerated lessons, projects, and other activities while the larger group is in session. Once the students and the team of teachers are together to create ideas and respond to shared needs and interests, the energy and enthusiasm and thus the possibilities are endless. Despite the heavy content orientation of the curriculum, the course then develops according to the people involved. It is they who create the environment of discovery by examining and experimenting, by redefining and rejuvenating the educational process and the school community.

BIBLIOGRAPHY

1. *Baroque Art and Music.* Filmstrip. Pleasantville, N.Y.: Educational Audio Visual, 1974.

2. Boyer, Ernest L. *High School: A Report on Secondary Education in America.* Carnegie Foundation for the Advancement of Teaching. New York: Harper and Row, 1983.

3. Chapman, Laura. *Instant Art, Instant Culture: The Unspoken Policy for American Schools.* New York: Teachers College Press, 1982.

4. Efland, Arthur D. "Excellence in Education: The Role of the Arts." In *Fine Arts in the Curriculum*, edited by Frederick B. Tuttle, Jr., pp. 11–15. Washington, D.C.: National Education Association, 1985.

5. Eisner, Elliot W. "Why Arts Are Basic." *Basic Education* 31, no. 9, May 1987.

6. Fowler, Charles B. "The Implications for the Arts of Recent Education Studies and Reports." In *Fine Arts in the Curriculum*, edited by Frederick B. Tuttle, Jr., pp. 56–63. Washington, D.C.: National Education Association, 1985.

7. Goodlad, John I., and Morrison, Jack. "The Arts in Education." *Design,* January/February 1982.

8. *K–12 Arts Education in the United States: Present Context, Future Needs: A Briefing Paper for the Arts Education Community.* Joint publication of Music Educators National Conference, National Art Education Association, National Dance Association, American Theatre Association, National Association of Schools of Music, National Association of Schools of Art and Design, National Association of Schools of Theatre, National Association of Schools of Dance. Reston, Va., January 1986.

9. Murray, Jon J. "Art, Creativity and the Quality of Education." In *Fine Arts in the Curriculum*, edited by Frederick B. Tuttle, Jr., pp. 23-30. Washington, D.C.: National Education Association, 1985.

10. Tuttle, Frederick B., Jr., ed. *Fine Arts in the Curriculum.* Washington, D.C.: National Education Association, 1985.

NEA POLICY
ON FINE ARTS EDUCATION

Resolution C-24. Fine Arts Education

The National Education Association believes that artistic expression is basic to an individual's intellectual, aesthetic, and emotional development. The Association therefore believes that every elementary and secondary school curriculum must include a balanced, comprehensive, and sequential program of fine arts instruction taught by educators certified in those fields.

The Association urges its state affiliates to become involved in the promotion, expansion, and implementation of a fine arts program in the curriculum. (80, 87)